Change Your Brain

by
Timothy Leary

Change Your Brain

by Timothy Leary
ISBN: 978-1-57951-017-6 E-ISBN: 978-1-57951-076-3
Copyright © 1988 by Timothy Leary
Deriviative Copyright 2000 by Beverly A. Potter

Published by
RONIN Publishing, Inc.
PO Box 3008
Oakland CA 94609
www.roninpub.com

Manuscript creation: Beverly Potter
Cover design: Judy July, Genertic Typography
Printed in the USA
Distributed by Perseus/PGW.

Library of Congress Card Number - 00-109751

This derivative was created by Beverly A.Potter, Ph.D. from Part Two of *Changing My Mind Among Others* (1982) by Timothy Leary.

Change Your Brain
by
Timothy Leary

Ronin Publishing
Berkeley, CA
roninpub.com

Timothy Leary books
Published by RONIN

Table of Contents

Introduction

The major theme of this book, repeated in every chapter, is neurologic, or neurophysics—the "scientizing" of internal experiences which, in the pre-scientific past, have been called psychological, spiritual, mystical, visionary, subjective, mental, sensory, esthetic-erotic, emotional, or religious.

From my first published paper in 1946, my obsession has been to objectify inner experiences, to demystify the software of human existence. How? By relating changes in external behavior, systematically and lawfully, to changes in the brain. Why? To give the individual, the Human Singularity, power over hir own internal experiencing, that is, power over hir brain and hir external behavior.

> My obsession has been to objectify inner experiences, to demystify the software of human existence

Achieving this required that we work the tissue frontiers, the membrane borders where the external traffics with the internal; where the outside world interfaces the antennae of the nervous system. For example, when we gave 100 micrograms of LSD to a subject—often one of ourselves—we were observing the effects of this measurable stimulus administered in a specified external setting on the receptive nervous system. We could not "see" the changes in the brain—yet!—but we could infer them during the acid-trip by measuring reactions in the form of questionnaires, reports, behavior. And, on the broader social scale, we could observe the effects on American culture of 7,000,000 people dropping acid. We observed the effect on those who tripped and those who did not—and the collision between the two swarms.

We work the tissue frontiers, the membrane borders where the external traffics with the internal; where the outside world interfaces the antennae of the nervous system.

Chapter 1

The Brain-Drug Option

A lmost everyone in the 1960's began popping brain-change pills to alter moods, perspectives, realities. From middle-class Valium addicts, to "reward-your-self-with-a-light-beer-after-work" drinkers, to pot-heads, over 80,000,000 Americans caught on that brain function can be changed by one simple behavior—put a specified chemical into your body.

Predictably enough, most of those who used drugs during the 1960s and 1970s glorified the drugs and raved incoherently about inner experiences, but failed to realize that the brain was the key. The very term "consciousness-expanding"—or "consciousness-altering"—drug is a primitive, prescientific concept. The precise terminology is brain-change-drug. We often preferred the term "brain-reward-drug." These verbal distinctions are not petty or pedantic. The Brain is the key. The Brain is the source. The Brain is God. Everything that humans do is Neuroecology.

The Brain is the key.

The Brain is the source.

The Brain is God.

In 1960 to 1961, a group of some 35 professors, instructors, and graduate students organized what later became the Harvard Psychedelic Research Project.

Core members of this influential task force included Walter Houston Clark, Houston Smith, Richard Alpert, Gunther Weil, Ralph Metzner, Walter Pahnke, Aldous Huxley, Alan Watts, George Litwin, Frank Barron. Among the part-time participants and advisors were Allen Ginsberg, William Burroughs, Arthur Koestler, Ken Kesey. Andrew Weil, Stanley Krippner, Al Hubbard, Gordon Wasson, Gerald Heard, Charles Olson, Jack Kerouac, Neal Cassady, Ken Babbs.

The historical impact of this "swarm" of influential scholars has not yet been recognized by the still-timid press

Vectored into the attitude of this extraordinary company were scientific enthusiasm, scholarly fervor, experimental dedication. Statistical morale was consistently high because the numbers looked so good.

Over 400 "subjects" shared high-dosage psychedelic experiences with the researchers in an atmosphere of esthetic precision, philosophic inquiry, inner search, self-confident dignity, intellectual openness, philosophic courage, and high humor. The historical impact of this "swarm" of influential scholars has not yet been recognized by the still-timid press—popular or scientific. The "Bloomsbury biographies" await a new generation.

Empirical Inquiry

The experimental methods and attitudes used were more important than the drugs. These neurological experiments were the first wide-scale, systematic, deliberate application to human behavior of the relativistic theories of particle behavior. Our research picked up precisely where the giant founders of experimental psychology—Wilhelm Wundt, Gustav Fechner, William James, Edward Titchener—left off a long generation before. Our aim, like theirs, was the precise correlation of objective-external differences with internal conscious reactions.

Forgotten in the later hysteria of the 1960's was the exquisite design of the early Harvard experiments. Rarely in the short history of psychology was such elegant, complex, socially influential research conducted! At the same time that the CIA was furtively dosing unwitting Harvard students for purposes of control and destruction, we were operating with the books wide open. No secrets, careful record keeping, pre/post testing. Triple-blind designs, total collaboration, the intensive training of "guides." The extensive publication of results in scientific journals—including that impressive model of scholarly innovation we called the Psychedelic Review.

Who Can Use Brain-Drugs?

From the first we were preoccupied with the classic question: Who gets to go? Who can select the brain-drug option? Our first answer as scientists was simply to publish our

Every pressure group wished the control-decisions to be made by itself.

results and let individuals, in dialogue with society, wrangle over the answer. But it was clear, immediately, that every pressure group wished the control-decisions to be made by itself. Physicians insisted that only those with MD's... police said no one... the older wished drugs kept from the younger.

Our second answer was that any and every informed adult democratic American should decide who and what to put in hir own body. The question, "Who should take acid?" was a repeat of the familiar, Who should have sex with whom? Who can smoke nicotine? Use alcohol? Wear bikinis? Drive a pleasure car? Transmit radio waves? In democracies, these personal decisions are made by individuals and cannot be ceded to officials, all too eager to meddle in individuals' affairs.

For the Elite Only

At Harvard, these decisions were not made quickly. Many of our advisors urged that the drugs should remain exclusive. Gerald Heard, of blessed memory, was the most outspoken elitist: "These sacraments are powerful tools for the guild of philosophers."

On the other side of the debate was Allen Ginsberg, the crusader for democratization, even socialization, of the drugs. Ever the worrying, nagging revolutionary, Allen howled his 1950's anarchic chant—"Turn on the world!"

Turn on the world!
—Allen Ginsberg

Play Ball with the Hive

There was a middle position: Play ball with the Hive Establishment. Stay on government or institutional payrolls—with tenure—and reassure the commissars that psychedelic drugs can somehow produce more efficient, well-adjusted, serene soviet workers. Use the drugs to advance our positions in the bureaucracy. On to HEW! On to Stockholm!

Freelance Gentlemen-Scholars

Curiously, the Harvard group never even considered this "mature" position. The most influential of our number were freelance gentlemen-scholars not dependent on any bureaucracy: Huxley, Alpert, Metzner, Heard, Ginsberg, Olson, Leary, Clark. And with few exceptions, our younger graduate students made the courageous decision to work outside the academic system. Another thought-provoking fallout from the Cambridge research—almost none of the graduate students "grew-up" to become conventional, tenured, academic pensioners.

> We human ethologists, activist anthropologists, left the Ivy Tower to live with the domesticated primates.

Domesticated Primates

As the world came to know, our 1963 decision was to expand our experimental design from selected laboratory samples of hundreds to field studies involving millions. We human ethologists, activist anthropologists, left the Ivy Tower to live with the domesticated primates.

Chapter 2

Scientizing the Internal

In pursuing my fervent goal of relating external stimuli to reports about internal-neural change, we were, paradoxically enough, following the most orthodox tradition in psychology. For performing experiments which the forgotten founders of scientific psychology would have understood and applauded, we were thrown out of Harvard and subjected to the Sernmetwels Treatment.

> For performing experiments which the forgotten founders of scientific psychology would have understood and applauded, we were thrown out of Harvard and subjected to the Sernmetwels Treatment.

Sir Isaac Newton

Scientific attempts to bridge the external and the internal were begun by Sir Isaac Newton, a recognized, eclectic master of the sciences of his day. When the University of London was closed for two years during the plague from 1664 to 1666, Newton "withdrew" from the outside world and discovered the laws of gravitation, the calculus. and the theory of the light spectrum. Shortly thereafter, Newton lost interest in measuring external events and turned most of his energies "towards alchemy, theology and history, particularly problems of chronology."

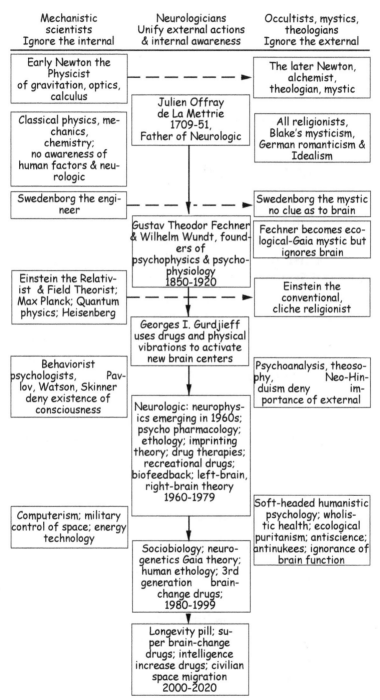

Mechanistic scientists Ignore the internal	Neurologicians Unify external actions & internal awareness	Occultists, mystics, theologians Ignore the external
Early Newton the Physicist of gravitation, optics, calculus		The later Newton, alchemist, theologian, mystic
Classical physics, mechanics, chemistry; no awareness of human factors & neurologic	Julien Offray de La Mettrie 1709-51, Father of Neurologic	All religionists, Blake's mysticism, German romanticism & Idealism
Swedenborg the engineer		Swedenborg the mystic no clue as to brain
Einstein the Relativist & Field Theorist; Max Planck; Quantum physics; Heisenberg	Gustav Theodor Fechner & Wilhelm Wundt, founders of psychophysics & psychophysiology 1850-1920	Fechner becomes ecological-Gaia mystic but ignores brain
		Einstein the conventional, cliche religionist
Behaviorist psychologists, Pavlov, Watson, Skinner deny existence of consciousness	Georges I. Gurdjieff uses drugs and physical vibrations to activate new brain centers	Psychoanalysis, theosophy, Neo-Hinduism deny importance of external
	Neurologic: neurophysics emerging in 1960s; psycho pharmacology; ethology; imprinting theory; drug therapies; recreational drugs; biofeedback; left-brain, right-brain theory 1960-1979	
Computerism; military control of space; energy technology		Soft-headed humanistic psychology; wholistic health; ecological puritanism; antiscience; antinukees; ignorance of brain function
	Sociobiology; neurogenetics Gaia theory; human ethology; 3rd generation brain-change drugs; 1980-1999	
	Longevity pill; super brain-change drugs; intelligence increase drugs; civilian space migration 2000-2020	

The old mind-body dilemma finally solved by neurologic.

Newton was a "Head"

In other words, at the peak of his scientific triumphs, Newton became a "head," a student of the inner spiritual world—or in modern terms, a neurologician. Modern physicists do not dwell on this dramatic life-change in their hero.

Gustav Fechner

After Newton's attempt to relate the external-material and the internal-spiritual, physics and chemistry became mechanistic. German Idealism with Immanuel Kant, British mysticism with William Blake, German Romanticism including Schopenhauer's renovation of oriental passivity, all reacted with revulsion from the scientific and tended to deny the importance, relevance, or even the existence of external movements. Thus, the brilliant significance of Fechner's attempts to apply the rigor of mechanistic and mathematical science to the richness of the subjective-inner-neurological.

Since the book you are now reading—and my life—is a faithful, dutiful, follow-up to the work and life of Fechner, it may be useful to summarize this philosophic giant's extraordinary career. Current psychological priesthoods ignore the fact that the profession of psychology was originated by Gustav Theodor Fechner, a physicist who recognized that the key to understanding human nature was the relationship between external stimuli and the brain.

Gustav Theodor Fechner (1801-87) became professor of physics at Leipzig in 1834, but ill health forced him to leave in 1839. His "illness" was clearly neurological or psychosomatic. He lay in bed for a year, unable to see, communicate, or locomote. This "sensory-social deprivation" ended one day when he rose, walked to the garden, looked around, and announced that all life was a unity. The rest of his career was devoted to "scientizing" the internal ineffable. Two of his most important books were Zend-Avesta (1851) and Elementen der Psychophysik (1860). He maintained that life is manifested in all objects in the universe which was a brilliant anticipation of the Gaia theory proposed by Lovelock and Margulis in 1978, and of the exobiological researches that were to transform science in the late 20th century.

Note that the origins of scientific psychology were called psychophysics and that Fechner wrote a book on psycho-esthetics. The importance of these concepts has been ignored by the mechanistic psychological bureaucracies that have domesticated psychology during the 20th century. The book you hold in your hand cannot be understood unless you grasp that the recent history of philosophy-science is nothing less than the ancient struggle to relate body and mind, i.e., the external-mechanistic with the internal-neurological.

Mechanistic psychological bureaucracies domesticated psychology during the 20th century.

Just Noticeable Differences

Brass-instrumented laboratories popped up in Germany, England, and America. Psychology was called "introspectionism." The subject used in experiments was a "trained introspectionist," i.e., one who could purify hir mind of extraneous thought and concentrate on "J.N.D.s" (Just Noticeable Differences) in external stimuli.

Which weight felt heavier? What were the discriminated units of perceived taste, smell, kinesthetic sensitivity? Sensational psychology. During the 1920s, Ivan Pavlov and John Broadus Watson glorified raw-radical mechanistic behaviorism and denied the existence of consciousness as a scientific datum. At the same time—and these polarities seem to be perfectly synchronized according to laws of cyclical development—Freud and his diverse followers focused on consciousness and unconsciousness.

Socialism, communism, and liberal-rationalism tended to stress the material. Right-wing thinkers stressed the romantic-spiritual. The caricature extreme of this polarity is illustrated by Hitler—a romantic vegetarian, a student of the occult, who believed in race, blood, soul, genetic-chauvinism, social Darwinism, destiny, drugs, vision. And on the other side, Stalin who killed 20,000,000 in the name of dialectical materialism, socialism, and economic progress, and Mao who killed 40,000,000 for the same cause.

The Head Trip

By 1960, both the psychoanalytic and the socialist-materialist dreams had begun to fade. Psychophysics boomed back with a bang—although now called neurophysics, more commonly known as the "head-trip."

Chapter 3

Psychedelic Conference
in Copenhagen

In the fall of 1959, I taught behavioral psychology at the University of Copenhagen by day, and by night learned experiential psychology in the port-town's psychlotrons. Eighteen months later, respectably perched at Harvard, I received a letter from a friend, a professor of psychology in Denmark. Copenhagen had been selected as host city for the 1961 convention of the International Association of Psychology.

My friend confided that Danish psychology was suffering from an inferiority complex in relation to medical psychiatry, and that the Psychology Department fervently hoped that the international congress would establish the credibility and respectability of psychology—thus resulting in increased federal funding.

> A psychlotron is an environment where human behavior is intensified, accelerated, charged with high-voltage— where the social molecular structures are dissolved so that the individual's behavior and the conclusions and interactions can more easily be observed and recorded.

The conference was scheduled in smorgasbord style—visiting psychologists had their choice of some 20 seminars or presentations at any time—except for the first day, which was devoted to three general convocations. Could I help in suggesting keynote speakers for the three plenary sessions? Sure thing, Bjorn.

History in the Making

We quickly agreed on a slam-bang opening day. The conference would open in the morning with a lecture by Harvard Professor Harry Murray—elegant, courtly, romantic, high cultural dean of personality psychology.

For the afternoon plenary, my suggestion of Aldous Huxley was enthusiastically accepted. The distinguished British author was a favorite of the anglophile Danes who knew him as a sophisticated novelist. As it turned out, the genial Danes were unaware that Huxley's recent books were devoted to consciousness-altering drugs.

The evening plenary session, chaired by me, focused on new methods of psychotherapy. In addition to my major lecture, there would be contributions by my brilliant, innovative friend-mentor Frank Barron, who had introduced me to the use of psychedelic drugs. Also scheduled was Richard Alpert, my partner in the Harvard Psychedelic Drug Project.

> I can't be left behind by romantic-literary upstarts like you and Huxley.
> —Harry Murray

Bohemian Influence

A few weeks before the conference, Professor Murray walked into my Harvard office with the congress schedule in his hand, chuckling: "You've subverted this sedate, boring conference into a wild bohemian drug session, haven't you?" I smiled and nodded.

"In that case," replied the suave Professor Murray, with a twinkle In his eye, "I guess you better guide me through one of your visionary trips. I can't be left behind by romantic-literary upstarts like you and Huxley." And so it came to pass that Professor Murray came to my home and, propelled by psilocybin mushrooms, voyaged to uncharted realms of his own neurology.

> **Covering the front page was a photo, magnified to 12 gleaming inches, of Richard Alpert's eye, dilated, popping out wildly.**

New Visions for Psychology

Professor Murray opened the congress by announcing that after taking a psychedelic trip he had shelved his prepared lecture in favor of a new topic: New Visions for Psychology's Future. Not a bad beginning! In the afternoon, Aldous Huxley took the enormous gathering of solemn-faced academicians through The Doors of Perception.

As we left the Queen's Palace Auditorium, three members of the Danish psychology faculty rushed up to me complaining bitterly and waving newspapers. One top headline read: I Was The First Scandinavian Reporter To Try The Poisonous Mushrooms From Harvard.

Covering the front page was a photo, magnified to 12 gleaming inches, of Richard Alpert's eye, dilated, popping out wildly. Underneath, the photo's caption read: "'I can control my insanity,' says Professor Alpert of Harvard."

It seemed that Richard Alpert—in later years to become a Hindu holy man, by the name of Baba Ram Dass—had the night before been partying with some members of the press and had been persuaded to turn on the reporter.

There was an innocence and excitement.

"You are making fools of us," shouted the Danish psychologists. "You Americans don't understand. Denmark is a very little, cozy, quiet country. Scientists are not supposed to perform experiments that are reported on the front page."

I reassured them that the evening's program would be impressive and history-making. And I promised them that during the congress, Richard Alpert would not turn on any more Danes.

Final Straw of Scientific Respectability

After scholarly presentations by Professor Frank Barron and another respectable psychologist, Richard Alpert walked to the podium and shocked the audience—me included!—by announcing that the visionary experience was an end in itself and that the drug-induced religious-mystical trip produced love, Christian (sic) charity, and the peace that passeth understanding.

This final straw broke the back of scientific respectability. Psychiatrists leaped up and, in seven languages, denounced nonmedical psychologists discussing drugs, and berated the notion of drugs used for growth instead of as cures for disease. For the angry psychiatrists, there was much applause.

At our hotel suite later we were joined by three Danish psychologists who looked at me with melancholy reproach. "You have set Danish psychology back twenty years."

"Not at all," I cried, filling their glasses with aquavit and their brains with positive electricity. "You have **I filled their glasses with aquavit and their brains with positive electricity.** just hosted the most important congress in the history of psychology. The annals of our science will record that in Copenhagen, psychology became a true science of brain change. I'll bet you a bottle of champagne that in twenty years this conference will be compared to those moments in history when Newton and Darwin spoke before the Royal Society." We continued abusing the dangerous Danish drug and left on good terms.

Two weeks later, in September 1961, further history was made at the annual meetings of the American Psychological Association. Acting as a moderator of a symposium on altered states of consciousness, I assembled a panel that included Alan Watts and William Burroughs in his first American public appearance.

A crowd of young psychologists listened and went home to use drugs to alter consciousness. There was an innocence and excitement that motivated these first proposals to change behavior by altering the brain with neurotrophic drugs.

Chapter 4

It's All a Game

Except for reflexes, instinctual reactions, and random muscular movements—which fall into the province of physiology—all behavior is imprinted by and conditioned by social pressures. Behavior sequences which are culturally determined might be considered game sequences. The listener may think I refer to "play," but I also consider stern, serious, real-life activities as "games." A game is defined as a learned cultural sequence characterized by six factors: Roles, Rules, Goals, Rituals, Language, and Values.

> **Human behavior can best be understood in terms of "games."**

Game Theory

That evening I delivered a lecture from the following material, which subsequently was reprinted in psychology textbooks and several reference volumes. It is considered a classic, influential work because it introduces the notion that human behavior can best be understood in terms of "games." For example, the position "husband" in the Game of Marriage is seen as comparable to a position of, say, "outfielder" in the Game of Baseball.

Game Theory is a very subversive, meta-social concept. It implies that you are not just the role that you—and society—have fabricated for you. It encourages flexibility, humorous detachment from social pressures. It allows you to change "games" and positions without the shame-stigma of being unreliable or undependable. It allows people to study and even measure their performances, and to seek coaching. It endorses change-ability and an amused-cynical liberation from "hive" pressures. Game Theory subtly undermines the cultural authoritarianism that forces people to play rigid parts in games that they themselves do not select.

Game Theory is a subversive, meta-social concept.

Another "historic" contribution of my presentation that night, and which follows here, is that it presented, for the first time, the notion that in order to change behavior or external performance, it is necessary to change your inner experience, ie., your neurology.

This was the first advocacy of brain-change drugs, not as medicines to cure disease, but as self-employed instruments to improve, change, and manage one's consciousness. Now it is an archeological curiosity.

Far from being frivolous, many so-called sports, or "play-games" are superior in their behavior-change techniques to psychiatry and psychology. The "game" of American baseball is superior to any so-called behavioral science. Baseball officials have classified and reliably record molecular behavior—bit sequences such as strikes, hits, double plays, and so forth. Their compiled records convert into indices for summarizing and predicting behavior, such as RBI or runs batted in; ERA or earned-run average, etc. To judge those rare events that are not obviously and easily coded, baseball employs well-trained umpires.

Baseball experts have devised another remarkable set of techniques for bringing about desired results: coaching. Baseball shares time and space with learners, sets up role models, feeds relevant information back to the learner, for endless practice. Baseball is clean and successful because it is seen as a game. You can shift positions. You know how you are doing. You can quit or declare yourself a free agent

Culture Is the Game Master

Cultural stability is maintained by preventing people from seeing that the Roles, Rules, Goals, Rituals, Language, and Values of society are game structures. Cultural institutions encourage the delusion that games have inevitable givens, involving unchangeable laws of behavior. Most cultures treat the family game as an implicit contract limited in time and space. It is treason not to play the nationality game, the racial game, the religious game.

The Behavior-Change Game

Like baseball and basketball, the behavior that psychiatrists label as "disease" can be considered a game, too. Dr. Thomas Szasz suggests that "hysteria" is a certain doctor-patient game involving deceitful helplessness. Psychiatry, according to this model, is a behavior-change game.

Psychotherapy is a medical game that interprets confusion and inefficiency in game-playing as illness.

The currently popular method of behavior change is called psychotherapy—a medical game that interprets confusion and inefficiency in game-playing as illness. Consider the football player who doesn't know the rules. Perhaps he picks up the ball and runs off the field. Shall we pronounce him sick and call the doctor? Not understanding the game nature of behavior leads to confusion and eventual helplessness.

When people come to us and ask us to change their behavior, we can find out what games they are caught up in, what games they want to commit themselves to. Expose them to models of successful game-playing, feed back objective appraisals of their performance. How do you care for them? Share time and space with them. Sounds simple enough, doesn't it?

The science game, the healing game, the knowledge game, are our proudest game accomplishments, but only as long as they are seen as games. When they go beyond this point, the trouble begins: the emergence

A person who can stand outside or above hir culture can often cut through games-rules to what is most relevant to survival and peace of mind.

of experts, professionals, priests, technocrats, status-bound engineers. At this point, games that began with the goal of decreasing human helplessness end up increasing it.

The most effective approach to behavior change is applied neurologic or self-programmed brain-change. Identify the game structure of the event. Make sure that you do not apply the rules and concepts of other games to this situation. Move directly to solve the problem. A person who can stand outside or above hir culture can often cut through games-rules to what is most relevant to survival and peace of mind.

Visionary Brain-Change

How can we Westerners see that our own potentials are much greater than the social-hive games in which we are so blindly trapped? Once the game structure of behavior is seen, change in behavior can occur with dramatic spontaneity.

The visionary brain-change, consciousness-altering experience is the key to behavior change. All the learned games of life can be seen as programs that select, censor, and thus dramatically limit the available cortical response.

> The visionary brain-change, consciousness-altering experience is the key to behavior change.

Acid Unplugs the Game

Consciousness-expanding drugs unplug these narrow programs, the social ego, the game-machinery. And with the ego and mind unplugged, what is left? Not the "id"; no dark, evil impulses. These alleged negative "forces" are, of course, simply taboos, anti-rules. What is left is something that Western culture knows little about—the uncensored cortex, activated, alert and open to new realities, new imprints.

Why is this brain-activating experience so strange and horrid to Western culture? Perhaps because our Western world is overcommitted to objective, external behavior games. This is a natural opposition and a healthy one: "The game" versus the "meta-game." Behavior versus consciousness. The universal brain-body versus the local cultural mind.

But this old paradox should be made explicit if it is to be fun. What should provoke intense and cheerful competition too often evokes suspicion, anger, impatience. Intelligence increase stimulated by brain-change is, to me, one of the greatest challenges of our times.

In three hours, under the right circumstances,

Those who talk about the games of life are seen as frivolous anarchists tearing down the social structure.

local games that frustrate and torment can be seen in the broader, evolutionary dimension. But in the absence of relevant scientific rituals to handle the drug experience, physicians seek to impose their game of control and prescription. Bohemians naturally impose their games of back-alley secrecy. Police naturally move in to control and prosecute.

Those who talk about the games of life are invariably seen as frivolous anarchists tearing down the social structure. Actually, only those who see culture as a game can appreciate the exquisitely complex magnificence of what human beings have done.

Those of us who play the game of "applied mysticism" respect and support good gamesmanship. You pick out your game, learn the rules, rituals, concepts; play fairly and cleanly. Anger and anxiety are irrelevant, because you see your small game in the context of the great evolutionary game which no one can lose.

Chapter 5

We Did Research

In our research endeavors we developed 11 egalitarian principles to determine role, rule, ritual, goal, language, value, and to define real, the good, the true, the logical. Any contract between humans should be explicit about any temporary suspension of these equalities. Two research projects attempted to put these egalitarian principles into operation.

Studying Brain-Change Experience

> They reported a sudden perception of the effects of abstractions, rituals, learned-game routines.

In one study we administered psilocybin, in a naturalistic supportive setting, in order to observe the rituals and language Americans impose on an intense brain-change experience quite alien to their culture. One hundred and sixty-seven subjects—43 females and 124 males—were given psilocybin. Of these, 26 were scholars, artists, medical doctors, professional intellectuals; 21 were nonprofessional normals, 27 were drug addicts with psychological or physical addiction; and 10 were inmates of a state prison. The drug was given only once, under informal, non-laboratory conditions, with no attempt to be therapeutic or problem oriented.

Changes Lives for the Better

Seventy-three percent of our subjects reported the psilocybin experience as "very pleasant" or ecstatic and 95% thought the experience had changed their lives for the better. Three out of four reported happy reactions. The most common reaction reported was the sudden perception of the effects of abstractions, rituals, learned-game routines. Subjects experienced ecstatic pleasure at being temporarily freed from these limitations.

Many of the 167 subjects in our study were already involved in rewarding games to which they could return with renewed vision and energy. But many of our subjects came through the psilocybin experience with the knowledge that they were involved in nonrewarding games, caught in routines they disliked. Many of them moved quickly to change their life games. For others, the "therapeutic" effect of the experience did not last. They were left with pleasant memories of their visionary journey and nothing more.

Prisoner Studies

There was not one moment of friction or tension.

The second experiment involved 35 volunteer prisoners in a maximum security prison. The recidivism rate was 80%. Twenty-eight would be expected back in prison within a year. In baseball terms, 80% is the error percentage our team attempted to lower.

The drug was given after three orientation meetings with the prisoners. The psilocybin session was followed by three discussions, then another drug session, then more discussions. In some 100's of hours of mind-blown interaction, there was not one moment of friction or tension.

Dramatic Results

Pre/post testing demonstrated dramatic decreases in hostility, cynicism, depression, schizoid ideation and definite increases in optimism, playfulness, flexibility, tolerance, sociability. The psilocybin experience made these men aware that they had been involved in stereotyped "cops and robbers" games—of being tough guys, of outwitting the law, of resentful cynicism. "My whole life came tumbling down, and I was sitting happily in the rubble." said one prisoner.

The group became a workshop for planning future games. Some prisoners were trained to take over the functions of a vocational guidance clinic—preparing occupational brochures for inmates about to be released, making plans to act as rehabilitation workers after their release and to organize a halfway house for ex-convicts. Other prisoners used their time to prepare for the family game, the old job games to which they would return.

> **People are upset when their games are changed.**

Cons Changed Their Games

Of course, our new game of allowing criminals to take over responsibility, authority, and prestige brings us into game competition with the professional middle class. If criminals are no longer criminals, where do the rest of us stand? People are upset when their games are changed.

Chapter 6

The Creative Experience

istorically, creativity is often associated with psychosis, alienation, and delinquency—The flaky artist, the mad scientist; even Einstein as lovable, absent-minded clown. Whenever 20th-century literature or film portrayed a brilliant mental giant who fabricated wonderful new realities, he was invariably a bad guy!

Recall the classic movie stereotype of the genius who builds gleaming cities under the sea, who outwits and neutralizes both the Soviet and American military—God knows we have all longed to do that!—who constructs luxurious cities in space filled with genetically superior women and men. These handsome

Hatred of the creative is a phobic taboo against change originating in the Prometheus myth.

geniuses, always in loving collaboration with slinky, well-dressed ladies, are the enemy (!) whom James Bond—a macho, unprincipled, ruthless Gordon Liddy-type CIA agent—is sent to destroy!

Distrust of the Creative

But the ultimate in superstitious, Ayatollah-type future-fear is the Frankenstein myth—a scientist of the primitive 19th century who created life! And now the name of Frankenstein, to the easily-spooked natives of

America, is synonymous with "monster." The historic origin of this hatred of the creative, this phobic taboo against change is, of course, the Prometheus myth. S/He who has the confidence and heroic daring to seize the future for humanity is punished by paranoid, jealous, frightened Gods.

Before the individualistic American republic, no human tribe, nation, or race has allowed a high percentage of creative deviance.

These negative, eerie images of the creative person are not accidental. The cultural distrust of the innovator is genetic in origin. Species survival logically requires that the large majority of the genetic castes necessary to keep the gene pool moving through time-space be docilely reproductive. An anthill or beehive would be weakened if too many ants came up with bright new ideas. Before the individualistic American republic, no human tribe, nation, or race has allowed a high percentage of creative deviance.

Creative Castes

Today, ethology—which represents our genetic confidence and skill in open, direct, observation of human behavior—and neuro-logic—our readiness to tamper with the brain—allows us to define creativity as a process easily amenable t change. Anyone who wants to, can be coached to behave more creatively. And you can learn how to alter your brain function to experience in novel ways.

Reproductive Reproducer

The first creative type is Reproductive Reproducer. There is no novel behavior, no fresh experience. In a fast-moving frontier niche like America this docile, normal cast probably comprises only 75% of the population.

You can choose to be noncreative—reproductive—in your behavior and noncreative in your brain activity—acting and experiencing within the narrow confines of your local culture or hive. If you are a bank teller or a young psychologist with ambitions, this is the better part of wisdom. Actually, one's ability to change social role—caste—and to change one's brain is determined or limited genetically. Each gene pool proba-

> **At times of migration, more creative performers and brain changers are obviously needed.**

bly produces members of the four creative castes in the exact proportions necessary to keep the gene pool surviving at any particular ecological niche and time. At times of migration, more creative performers and brain changers are obviously needed.

Reproductive Creator

The Reproductive Creator can be more inventive in behavior, and yet remain docilely stereotyped in experiencing. A crafty skill in producing new combinations of old cultural stereotypes can be developed. Here we include artists, designers, entertainers, packagers who recycle old fads or add new wrinkles to the classics: "Hey, let's make Romeo and Juliet black and gay!" "Let's have the good guy turn out to be the bad guy!" "Let's raise the hemlines next year!" "Let's throw long on first down!" Wow! What creativity!

In a wide-open, mobile society like America, perhaps 12% of the population operates at this level. In a static society like Saudi Arabia, you will, of course, be drawn and quartered for suggesting even the slightest change in hemlines or in good-guy roles.

Creative Reproducer

The Creative Reproducer is an interesting and little discussed human caste which includes psychics, visionaries, idiot savants, those with unusual talents, Bobby Fischers, people with perfect musical pitch, mental calculators, intuitives, natural artists, and "oddballs."

In some past cultures, these people, whose brains are wired differently from the species norm, who see things differently, were recognized, tolerated, even rewarded. In most closed societies, these "strange ones" are ridiculed, ostracized, even punished. Demographic statistics on deviance suggest that 12% of any gene pool are exceptionally endowed. Their brains have activated futique circuits that would be optimal in some future or different niche, but which, in the present, put them naggingly out of touch.

> **In most closed societies, these "strange ones" are ridiculed, ostracized, even punished.**

Although Creative Reproducer brains are fabricating original realities, they use conventional-reproductive behaviors to express their visions. An Inquisition zealot looks through Galileo's telescope and declares that Satan's work is on display! A worried cardiologist takes LSD, activates ecstatic visceral circuits, and shouts that he is having a heart attack.

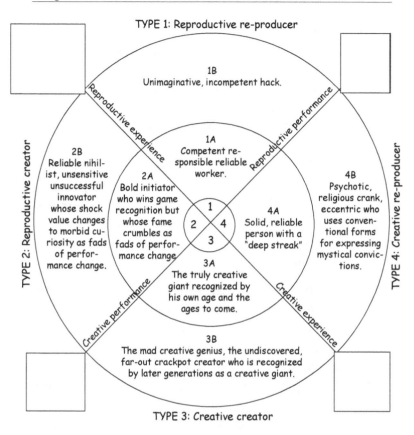

TYPE 1: Reproductive re-producer

1B
Unimaginative, incompetent hack.

1A
Competent re-
sponsible reliable
worker.

2B
Reliable nihil-
ist, unsensitive
unsuccessful
innovator
whose shock
value changes
to morbid cu-
riosity as fads
of perfor-
mance change.

2A
Bold initiator
who wins game
recognition but
whose fame
crumbles as
fads of perfor-
mance change.

4A
Solid, reliable
person with a
"deep streak"

4B
Psychotic,
religious crank,
eccentric who
uses conven-
tional forms
for expressing
mystical convic-
tions.

3A
The truly creative
giant recognized by
his own age and the
ages to come.

3B
The mad creative genius, the undiscovered,
far-out crackpot creator who is recognized
by later generations as a creative giant.

TYPE 2: Reproductive creator

TYPE 4: Creative re-producer

Reproductive experience

Reproductive performance

Creative performance

Creative experience

TYPE 3: Creative creator

Schematic diagrams of social labels used to describe types of
creativity. The inner circle illustrates positive social labels and
the outer circle illustrates negative labels.

If you have altered your brain to new revelation and
are running around using traditional metaphors, you
are undoubtedly a Creative Reproducer. If you have a
sense of humor, you are a joy and a delight. If lacking
in whimsy, you are a social bore and pious irritant. In
either case, you are advised to move to the last caste.

Creative Creator

The Creative Creator possesses an activated brain and has accepted the Heisenberg Determinacy—your brain is God the Fabricator—and can carpenter new realities in harmony with the fast swirl of current evolution. The Creative Creator fuses—uses appropriate cliches of the past, the trendiest waves of the present, technologies of the future. As suggested in our discussion of Creative Reproducers, access to "special" brain circuits is, for the most part, genetic. Genius does come from the genes.

Your brain is God the Fabricator.

A person in any of these four quadrants of creativity can be seen as effective or as incompetent by his culture—and, for that matter, by cultural subgroups. If we divided each type into those labeled by their contemporaries as (A) effective and (B) ineffective, we obtain the eight categories. These two-dimensional circular grids can plot test scores or content-analysis indices along the two coordinates in order to diagnose the individual. This system lends itself to the same variety of multilevel applications as the interpersonal circle which is explained in The Politics of Self-Determination.

Chapter 7

The Creativity Game

n most of life's crucial games we stumble in the dark, not knowing how we're doing. The first step in behavior change, then is explicit definition of the game, learning the rules and the strategies. You need some way of scorekeeping and to be at the proper space-time ballpark, hanging around people who are adepts at the game.

It is disappointing to come thundering over the goal line for a touchdown only to be greeted with yawns because the gang is playing tennis. I have spent a good part of my professional life doing this, by the way. Get a good coach. Behavior, being movement in space/time, is not changed by words or by repeating mistakes. And practice is needed.

> Get a good coach.

Researching Creative Set

In 1961 Frank Barron, William Meyers, who was a Harvard graduate student at the time, and I initiated a creativity-change project which allowed a preliminary crude check on these hypotheses. By matching pairs of students on faculty ratings of creativity, 40 volunteer subjects of the junior class at the Rhode Island School of Design were divided into groups A-authoritarian and C-creative, whose creativity ratings had equal means and equal standard deviations. IQ scores were available on all subjects.

First, both groups were administered, under identical conditions, the Guilford Unusual Uses Test and the Barron Originality, Independence of Judgment, and Preference for Complexity questionnaires, in that order. Then, after an intermission, the groups were separated.

The Creative group was asked to "play the role of an extraordinarily original and creative person". Group A-Authoritarian was asked to play the role of a highly intelligent authoritarian person. Both groups then repeated the tests. The results indicated that the Creative group improved in performance relative to the Authoritarian group on ability to think up ideas.

Creative Set Increases Creativity

This indicates that the creative set increases creative performance and the authoritarian set decreases creative performance. We may conclude that creativity can be increased. It also suggests that role playing, or set-taking, is a specific mechanism for increasing creativity.

Creativity has a social aspect as well, as shown by the results on the three Barron questionnaires that measure interpersonal and social attitudes. With the creative set, the Creative group increased its scores over its earlier scores with standard instructions. The Authoritarian group with the authoritarian set decreased its scores on the Barron questionnaires. Mind sets affecting creative performance also affected interpersonal and social orientation.

Authoritarian set decreases creative performance.

Creative Behavior is a "Game"

The results suggest that (1) creative behavior is a game sequence; (2) people have considerable voluntary control over their creative behavior; and (3) if the game contract is made explicit, behavior will change drastically in the direction that roles and goals demand. The experiment also suggests that people automatically shift rituals, adjust new rules, and employ the appropriate language once the commitment is made.

A sample of 50 juniors was selected at random for a feedback study. Barron and I met with each subject, opened the test folder, and explained the creativity test results. In every case we found **Why be a tortured genius, sacrificing a good income for risky bohemian independence?** that the students creativity scores and ratings of originality by faculty members checked closely with the stated game goals.

For instance, teachers rated one student with low originality scores as solid, responsible, but unimaginative, consistently indicating close identification with middle-class family values. From this student's subsequent discussion emerged this message: "I'm a normal, conventional person looking forward to a steady, interesting job and a happy family life. I've no desire to be a tortured genius, sacrificing a good income for risky bohemian independence."

There seemed little discrepancy between the level of creativity and professional goals selected. Painters and sculptors scored higher on independence of judgment, spontaneous flexibility, and social deviance than architects or industrial designers.

Activation of Creative Awareness

Researchers administered psilocybin to more than 400 persons, many of whom were financially dependent on being creative. Artistic and literary folks respond ecstatically and wisely to drug experience. They tell us this is what they have been looking for—new, intense, direct confrontation with the world about them.

Poets and painters have always tortured themselves to transcend space/time boundaries by every

> **Artistic and literary folks look for new, intense, direct confrontation with the world about them.**

means possible, and at certain historical time-places—invariably when political-economic security allows breathing space from survival pressures—entire cultures "get high" on brain-change techniques.

In the Khajuraho culture (c. A.D. 1000) an entire society collaborated in constructing enormous temples covered with erotic carvings. The Konark culture (c. 1250) again mobilized the energies of a generation in constructing acres of sexually explicit temple sculpture. A similar thing happened during the Mogul period, 17th century, in north India, when the Taj Mahal and other esthetic-erotic constructions dominated social consciousness. The prevalence of mind-changing drugs—several Mogul emperors were notorious hashish-opium smokers—and mind-changing yogic methods undoubtedly stimulated these amazing peaks of artistic expression.

Prisoners Became Spiritual

More than 100 psilocybin sessions run in a maximum-security prison demonstrated that creative vision and mystical illumination are a function of the cortex when it is temporarily relieved of word and ego games. More than half our semi-literate prisoners reported in blunt, nonabstract words what have to be interpreted as mystical experiences.

A lower class, uneducated criminal can, via psilocybin, experience what Blake saw in his visions. It's all there in the cortex after all. But the convict does not have language or literary skills to communicate his vision: "Yeah, Doc. I saw all these flames of fire, and, wow, I knew it meant

Lower class, uneducated criminals experienced what Blake saw in his visions.

the end of me, but then, I realized it can't really hurt because we're all part of the same thing anyway so I relaxed and went into it, and...." Reports like this come from the most verbal of our prisoner group. The majority just look us in the eye, shake their heads in awe, and say, "Gee, Doc, those mushrooms are really something out of this world."

New Combinations

We obviously cannot wait fifteen years while the prisoner finishes graduate work in English Literature and learns the literary game. But we can coach him in the creative production of new combinations. I think it is possible to get deep creative insights into whatever behavior sequence or professional occupation you are involved in.

Creativity is not a function of lucky heritage or elite training. There are more visions in the cortex of each of us than in all the museums and libraries of the world. There is a limitless possibility of new combinations of the old symbols.

There are more visions in the cortex of each of us than in all the museums and libraries of the world.

A true democracy of creativity—experienced and performed —is close at hand. Intensely close relationships develop among most people who have had this experience together. In the past, when these visionary experiences were accidental, a Dominican Father in Spain had his experience in one century, and a Hindu on the bank of the Ganges in another century—communication did not exist. And because disciplined mystic experience involves a withdrawal from games and social interaction, your monastic or hermit doesn't have people around. The group drug experience allows this to happen.

Chapter 8

Get Out of Your Mind

In 1964, the first commercial book summarizing LSD experimentation was edited by David Solomon, an early pioneer in psychedelic drug research who served a cruelly long sentence in an English prison for manufacture of LSD. The British judge who sentenced Solomon justified the Turkish barbarism on the grounds that Solomon had influenced millions of minds through his writings about drugs. This 20th century scholar was jailed for his ideas! Reflect for a moment on the melancholy fact that a pioneer scholar languished in prison for, among other things, publishing the book for which much material presented here was used in its introduction.

> **A bourgeois hysteria about recreational drugs convulsed the United States.**

Many ethologists have noted that in dealing with cultural change, British and Western European countries run about ten years behind America. The bourgeois hysteria about recreational drugs that convulsed the United States during the Nixon administration has now moved eastward to 20th-century Europe, where police officials and moralists have a new victimless crime to persecute.

Our team made three important contributions to neuro-logic. Major was the Motto: To use your head you have to go out of your mind which solves the classic dilemma of prescientific psychology and philosophy. We cannot study the brain, the instrument for fabricating the realities we inhabit, using the mental constructs of the past.

Visionary plants like the peyote cactus, the divine mushrooms of Mexico; divinatory vines and roots have been used for thousands of years. Today's technology provides synthetics of the active ingredients of these ancient and vulnerable concoctions. These foods and drugs produce ecstasy, the most sought after and most dread experience known to man. Ex-stasis means, literally, out of, or released from a fixed or unmoving condition. Some theorists like to suppose a steady growth in human consciousness; others, especially Eastern philosophers, point to alternating cycles of expansion and contraction and warn that man's awareness may contract down to the robot narrow precision of certain overorganized species of life. The anthill and the computer remind us that increased efficiency does not necessarily mean expanded awareness. I believe psychedelic drugs and their effects should be viewed in the context of this emergent philosophy of evolution of intelligence.

We cannot study the brain, the instrument for fabricating the realities we inhabit, using the mental constructs of the past.

Lord of All Species

The Renaissance-Reformation mythos would have us believe man is the chosen lord of all species. But in the last few decades, scientific instrumentation has confronted man with visions, vistas, and processes that have thoroughly dissipated hir philosophic securities. Astronomers speak of billions of light years, physicists of critical nuclear-process structures that last only microseconds. The genetic blueprinting strands are so compact that the seed of every human being on earth today could be contained in a box 1/8 inch on a side. The new scientific data define man as an animal only dimly aware of the energies and wisdom surrounding and radiating through hir.

> Our present mental machinery cannot possibly handle the whirling, speed-of-light, trackless processes of our brain, our organ of consciousness itself.

We can use our rational faculties to change our instruments and language, invent new mathematics and symbols to deal with processes beyond our neurological scope. But then comes the neurological implosion. Rational consciousness is a fragile, tissue-thin artifact easily blown away by the slightest alteration of biochemistry, by the simplest external stimulation—for example, by a few microvolts strategically introduced into specific areas of the brain, or by the removal of accustomed stimulation.

The potential of cerebral association is of the order of thirteen billion to the twenty-five-thousandth power, per second. But we think rationally at a maximum rate of three concepts—ten phonemes—a second. Our present mental machinery cannot possibly handle the whirling, speed-of-light, trackless processes of our brain, our organ of consciousness itself.

Being uncertain, ready to spin out unproven hypotheses is a sign of the preliminary, rapidly changing speculation that inevitably characterizes a new breakthrough in the realm of ideas.

The Paradox

To use our heads, to push out beyond words, space-time categories, social identifications, models and concepts, it becomes necessary to go out of our generally rational minds. If we at times seem uncertain, too ready to spin out unproven hypotheses, this is a sign of the preliminary, rapidly changing speculation that inevitably characterizes a new breakthrough in the realm of ideas.

Chapter 9

Our Epoch Is Mythos

It is useful to see all cultural institutions as expressions of the epoch's basic mythos; each discipline simply reorchestrating underlying themes of the age. What fails to fit the mythic harmonic tends to be heard as disruptive dissonance.

Thomas S. Kuhn describes how scientific activities are determined by paradigm—a distinctive world view—defining the problems and methods of any era. Science cannot go beyond the paradigm's limits without risking being seen as eccentric, even "unscientific." During the last fifty years our basic world view seems to have been undergoing another of these gigantic struggles of

What fails to fit the mythic harmonic tends to be heard as disruptive dissonance.

ideologies of which the current controversy over psychedelic drugs is but a minor skirmish. That our research provokes fierce controversy suggests that man's accepted view of himself is coming into collision with new concepts.

Classic View

The older, classic world view concerns itself with equilibria among forces that are visible, external, predictable, measurable, manageable by man, within the realm of macroscopic consciousness. The religious expression of this mythos is Protestantism, with its emphasis on behavior, achievement, balancing, and rationality. Democracy, communism, parliamentarianism, all emphasize the macroscopic, visible aspects of behavior.

Classic physical science emphasized the orderly; God the master engineer balancing the clockwork equilibrium of material forces. But the metaphorical interpretations we impose betray our implicit, basic commitments, which are usually unconscious: God runs the universe the way a good Christian runs his business; the way Andrew Mellon ran the country—like a factory.

> The metaphorical interpretations we impose betray our implicit, basic commitments, which are usually unconscious.

Psychology Fits the Myth

Psychology again fits the dimensions of the myth. Behaviorism—a scientific movement invented and manned by Protestants—recognizes only visible actions. Human personality is pictured as ruled by conservation principles—ego, id, superego—pushing toward equilibrium. There was much more to Freud than this, but the Hasidic, expansive, and mystical aspects of Freud's thinking have not survived the post-Freudian Protestantization of the theory.

The Emergent-Root Myth

Evidence from every branch of science testifies to energies and structures which, though fantastically potent, are microscopic—indeed, invisible. The good old macroscopic world is a rather clumsy, robotlike level of conception. Structure becomes process. Matter becomes a **Older views of man, defined in externals and behaviorals, are reaching an agonizing end-point.** transient state of energy. Stasis becomes ex-stasis.

The same exponential mythos appears in other institutions. Overproduction, overkilling, overpopulation, automation, remind us that older economic, political, religious, artistic, psychological views of man, defined in externals and behaviorals, are reaching an agonizing end-point.

Psychology, man's view of his nature, is always the last **Psychology, man's view of his nature, is always the last to adopt a new world view.** to adopt a new world view. From the standpoint of established values, the psychedelic process is dangerous and insane—a deliberate psychotization, a suicidal undoing of the equilibrium man should be striving for. With its internal, invisible, indescribable phenomena, the psychedelic experience is incomprehensible to a rational, achievement-oriented, conformist philosophy. But to one ready to experience the exponential view of the universe, psychedelic experience is exquisitely effective preparation for the inundation of data and problems to come.

Anatomical Structure of Consciousness

Each of us possesses around 30 billion brain cells, several times the number of human beings in the world. Each brain cell is a computer capable of relating with as many as 25,000 others. The number of possible associations is of the order of 30 billion to the twenty-five-thousandth power, a quantity larger than the number of atoms in the universe. This electrical-chemical complexity is the anatomical structure of consciousness.

> **Into the brain, each second, there pour something like 100 million sensations.**

Into the brain, each second, there pour something like 100 million sensations. The brain itself fires off around five billion signals a second. Yet we are aware of only the millionth fraction of our own cortical signaling. Huge areas of the brain—neurologists call them "silent areas"—are blocked off from consciousness. Reflective neurologists pose disturbing questions: "… has man, perhaps, more brain than he knows what to do with? Is his huge 'neo-pallium' like a powerful engine in a decrepit automobile that can never utilize more than a fraction of the available horsepower?"

Chapter 10

Imprinting

Imprinting was discovered by animal ethologists. Almost all we learn about human nature has and will come from our study of other species. We had to understand evolution of other species before we were bold enough to say—and how many dare say it today?—that humans evolve and that individual humans evolve at different rates. The concept of imprinting was applied to human development for the first time in the early 1960's in an essay based upon material that follows.

> **Imprinting is the selection of triggers that automatically activate inborn characteristics of the species.**

As the human being matures, different neural circuits are activated and the following neuro-technologies emerge in a predictable sequence: sucking, biting, crawling, walking, muscular domination, non-verbal social communication, imitation of symbols, invention of symbols, cooperative symbol communication, adolescent sexual-mating, parenting, and aging/security-seeking.

Imprinting, a biochemical freezing of external awareness, is confined to definite brief periods in individual life, and to a particular triggering set of environmental circumstances. Once accomplished, it is very stable—perhaps irreversible. It is often completed long before the specific behaviors which the imprinted pattern establishes. Imprinting is the selection of triggers that automatically activate inborn characteristics of the species.

Serial imprinting means that you can use your own brain as a movie camera to "shoot" the realities you inhabit.

As each brain circuit is activated, it blindly imprints the environmental cues that happen to be present. When the verbal imitative circuits are turned on around ages three to four, the language and mentation skills of the parents and custodians are-imprinted. If the child is Chinese, a Chinese mental reality is in-habituated. The first powerful sex object has an unshakable effect on further sexual conditioning. Even more interesting is the suggestion that imprints can be suspended and changed. Serial imprinting means that you can use your own brain as a movie camera to "shoot" the realities you inhabit.

Little is known about the learning processes by which the brain's enormous potential is limited and contracted. According to psychologist Clifford Morgan,

> [Konrad Lorenz] *happened to be present when some goose eggs in an incubator hatched. For this reason he was the first large moving object the goslings saw. Much to his surprise, the goslings began following him about as though he were their parent. The young*

goslings, in fact, would have nothing to do with their mother goose and insisted on his constant company. This learning takes place very rapidly and without any specific reward.... The imprinting phenomenon... can take place only during a short interval (a few hours or a day or two) and at a certain time (usually shortly following birth). It also seems irreversible; difficult to alter through subsequent learning. However, some true learning [may be] connected with it. Young goslings, for example, at first follow any human being [who] has been the first object contact after hatching. A few days later, however, they learn the individual characteristics of the person who ordinarily leads them to food and shelter, and then they will follow no one else. Thus imprinting may be a natural stage in maturation.

Here is a sudden irreversible learning, which seems independent of motivation, reward, conditioning—a sudden, shutter-like fixing of the nervous system. Once taken, the picture then determines the scope and type

Imprinting, a biochemical event, sets up the chessboard upon which slow, step-by-step conditioning takes place.

of subsequent "lawful learning." Imprinting, a biochemical event sets up the chessboard upon which slow, step-by-step conditioning takes place.

Eccentric Imprinting

One awesome aspect of imprinting is its unpredictable, accidental quality. In another experiment, young birds were presented with a Ping-Pong ball at the critical moment and spent their remaining lives pursuing plastic globes. This amusing and frightening experiment reminds us that each of us perceives the world through biochemical-neurological structures accidentally laid down in our earliest moments. We may be chasing the particular Ping-Pong ball which, at those sensitive moments, has been imprinted on our cortical film.

As the result of eccentric imprinting, fowl attempt to court humans; lambs desert the flock and follow **Which orange basketball imprinted you?** their keepers; goslings attempt to hatch watermelons; buffalo calves attempt to mate with huntsmen's horses; zebra foals attach themselves to moving cars; ducklings reject the mother in favor of orange basketballs.

The rather terrifying implication is that early, accidental, and involuntary events can tenaciously couple human instinctual machinery to entirely inappropriate stimuli. Another possibility is that all subsequent learning centers around the original imprint.

Serotonin

Some current neurological research already indicates that serotonin is a key factor in the transmission of nerve impulses. There is a difference in serotonin metabolism between infants and adults and between "normal" and schizophrenic persons. LSD also affects serotonin metabolism. Marplan, a drug which "builds up the brain's stockpile of serotonin," has a tranquilizing effect on mental patients, and blocks the action of LSD.

Serotonin might contribute to the imprinting process necessary for "normal" perception. The shifting, unfixed imagery of the involuntary—and unpleasant—psychotic state, and the voluntary—ecstatic—psychedelic state, are associated with a change in the body's serotonin level.

The Psychological Situation

A most confusing aspect of psychedelic drug phenomena is the wide variation of responses. There is the common factor of going beyond the imprinted, learned structure, but the specific content of what comes next is always different. LSD, mescaline, and psilocybin simply do not produce a generally predictable sequence of responses.

Psychedelic substances have negligible somatic effects. Their site of action is the higher nervous system—consciousness changes.

Once "normal" modes of awareness are suspended, specific consciousness changes occur due to set and setting.

Chapter 11

Hooked on Externals

Before the addicted "dope fiend" or alcoholic can be cured, he must recognize his affliction. The first step, therefore, is to recognize that our consciousness is totally hooked to certain externals; recognize the limits and directions of our imprints.

Some forms of psychoanalysis aim to do this. Long chains of associations are laboriously traced, step by step, to the original imprint situation. A new sequence of associations is attempted, centering on the person of the analyst—what Freudians call "transference." But, as Freud saw, verbal interaction in the consulting room cannot duplicate the impact of the original biochemical structuring. Each external imprint is uniquely located in space and time.

The human cut off from hir addictive "supply" of external stimuli shows all the symptoms of a "dope fiend"— restlessness, discomfort, anxiety.

Mental life is limited to associations relating back to the original imprint. The human being is "hooked" to the specific external stimulus. Sensory deprivation experiments suggest that the human cut off from hir addictive "supply" of external stimuli shows all the symptoms of a "dope fiend"—restlessness, discomfort, anxiety.

The brain is a motion-picture camera capable of shooting millions of frames a second. The imprint system is one of these frames, stopped—one static model, years out of date, kept current only by slow conditioning and association.

The "dead," "removed" quality of man's thinking has interested philosophers for centuries, and has been described most effectively by linguists and semanticists, especially Ludwig Wittgenstein, Edward Sapir, Benjamin Whorf, and Alfred Korzybski. What happens, outside or inside, we perceive in terms of our mental imprint system. We live in a frozen world—cut off from the flow of life and energy.

Imprinting equips us, cues us to maneuver around the neighborhood, determining attractions and repulsions. The genetic blueprint plays a statistical game. In spite of the occasionally freaky nature of many early imprints, enough of us do imprint appropriate stimuli that we reproduce, keep the hive-society going, and care for our young—the crucial genetic issues.

Suspension of Imprints

That the consciousness of prescientific humanity was limited to a tunnel vision may be of no consequence in the evolution of intelligence. When it's backbone time, it backbones. When it's brain-change time, species learn to reimprint.

All neurological processes are biochemical, and many experiments have demonstrated that imprinting can be postponed, altered, or prevented entirely by tension-reducing or tranquilizing drugs.

> **When it's brain-change time, species learn to reimprint.**

Certain alkaloid molecules, such as psychedelic drugs, dramatically suspend the conditioned, learned aspects of the nervous system. Suddenly released from its conditioned patterning, consciousness is flung into a flashing loom of unlearned imagery, an eerie, novel landscape where everything seems possible and nothing remains fixed. Might we consider the psychedelic effect as a temporary suspension of imprinting?

Psychedelic drugs may provide the possibility of reimprinting—a neurological restatement of the "death-rebirth" experience so often reported during psychedelic moments. During the psychedelic session, the subjects nervous system is in a disorganized flux closely analogous to that of infancy. And here we come to the accelerated personality change, rapid learning, sudden life changes so regularly reported by psychedelic researchers.

> **Psychedelic drugs may provide the possibility of reimprinting—a neurological restatement of the "death-rebirth."**

This chemical resuscitation of the frozen symbol systems is not a recent development. In every culture in recorded history, men have used chemicals of vegetable origin to alter consciousness. Members of cultures with primitive technologies and distribution systems will drop any activity in order to "get high." The same is true of cultures where primitive legal or moral sanctions make it difficult to obtain brain changers. During American Prohibition, a mass mania sprang up around liquor. The same is true in penitentiaries or in military servitudes.

Alcohol is primitive, crude, and dangerous; its worldwide popularity is probably due to European engineering methods for mass production and distribution. Alcohol, by the 18th century was available; other competing mind-changers were relatively rare.

The global popularity of chemical mind-changers is due to their producing ecstasy, perceptual change, fresh sensation. Ecstasy means to break out of the verbal prisons, suspend your imprints, see things anew, perceive directly.

With freshened perception goes the feeling of liberation, insight, the exultant sense of having escaped the lifeless net of symbols. Men drink, smoke, chew, or fast to

> **Men drink, smoke, chew, or fast to escape the tyranny of words, the limits of the imprint.**

escape the tyranny of words, the limits of the imprint; to regain what they have lost in socialization. The ecstatic is wordless. Try to describe even the mundane effect of getting "tight" at a cocktail party.

Reimprinting

What happens after the neurological liberation? How is it integrated back into life? Hinduism and Hinayana Buddhism flatly urge their devotees to reach a state of detached nirvana and stay there. Other philosophers have argued that ecstasy must lead to liberated return. Christian mystics, Mahayana Buddhists, and many Hindu sects insist that the person liberated from his neurological straitjacket will be known by his works and his actions.

Freedom from Imprints

But until recently, very few persons have actually attained freedom from imprints. Breathing exercises, monastic withdrawal, prolonged meditation, mantras, mudras, mandalas can produce a state of quietude and serenity, but only rarely do non-drug adepts report the blinding illumination, **But again, so what?** whirling inundation of accelerated sensation, unity through multiplicity, that characterize direct neurological confrontation. Today, by ingesting a psychedelic drug, temporary freedom from imprints is almost guaranteed. But again, so what?

Psychedelic Reimprint

These compounds produce new imprints. During a psychedelic session, the nervous system, stripped of all previous learning, is completely vulnerable. Powerful attachments and repulsions develop during psychedelic sessions. Here is the danger and promise of psychedelic drugs—the development of new symbol systems and the refocusing of old systems.

Chapter 12

Set and Setting

Development of the concept of "set and setting" is the third epic contribution that our wayward band of neuronauts made in those early years. Set refers to what the subject brings to the situation, hir earlier imprinting, learning, emotional and rational predilections, and, perhaps most important, his immediate expectations about the drug experience. Setting refers to the social, physical, emotional milieu of the session.

Before the 1960's, physicians and experimenters administered drugs in a most primitive, naive manner. It was assumed that each drug acted mechanically to bring about a specific physiological result. The placebo effect was recognized as a terrible stumbling block in the neat-precise mechanical science of determining how drug X influenced organ Y. Subjects given a sedative and told it was an energizer ran around restlessly and couldn't sleep. Subjects given energizers and told they were sleeping pills proceeded to nod out. These results used to plague researchers working for the big drug firms. The influence—indeed, the dominance—of the nervous system as managing our biocomputer was unheard of.

> **Drugs were administered in a most primitive, naive manner, assuming each drug acted mechanically to bring about a specific result.**

You cannot sensibly talk about the effects of a psychedelic drug without specifying the set of the subject and the environmental context. If both are supportive of self-discovery and aesthetic-philosophic inquiry, a life-changing experience results. If both are negative, a hellish encounter can ensue. Of course, people tend to impose familiar games onto the psilocybin experience. If the drug-giving person is supportive, flexible, and secure, then the experience is almost guaranteed to be pleasant and therapeutic.

The hypothesis we developed at Harvard suggested that the effect of any psychoactive drug was almost entirely due to the drug-taker's expectations and subjective assumptions interacting with the pressure of the environment. Even

If what we expect affects what happens in our brain, then let us precisely program the suggestions our vulnerable brain will realize.

in the primitive times of 1964, we were coming to realize that the brain is a robot computer perfectly designed to fabricate any reality we program it to construct. If you believe that LSD is lethal poison, even your ecstatic sensory orgasm will feel like a death convulsion. If, at that vulnerable sensitive moment of imprint suspension, the environment tells you that you are sick or in danger, your robot computer will so react.

Heisenberg Principle

Set and setting and the placebo effect demand that psychology get hip to the Heisenberg principle of determinancy. If what we expect affects what happens in our brain, then let us precisely program the suggestions our vulnerable brain will realize. If the setting also affects what happens in our brain, let us make sure that the environment is the reality we wish to inhabit. The brain is not a blind, reactive machine, but a complex, sensitive biocomputer that we can program. And if we don't take the responsibility for programming it, then it will be programmed unwittingly by accident or by the social environment.

Most important is the behavior, understanding, and empathy of the persons who first administer the drug and who remain with the taker while the drug is in effect. The psychedelic controversy itself is a broad social confirmation of the set-setting hypothesis.

The extreme suggestibility, the heightened vulnerability to internal or external stimuli points to the critical importance of expectation and environmental pressure.

The extreme suggestibility, the heightened vulnerability to internal or external stimuli—which leads some to paranoia, others to cosmic ecstasy—points to the critical importance of expectation and environmental pressure.

Chapter 13

Communicating Visionary Experiences

Words are inadequate to describe the speed, breadth, and shuttling flow of a 30-billion-cell cerebral computer—and the fears aroused by the very nature of the topic. Richard Alpert, Ralph Metzner and I gave a lecture to the staff of The Hudson Institute, one of the country's most respected think tanks. About thirty-five scientists were present, and in closing the meeting, the chairman—a well-known physicist who had taken LSD several times—questioned the possibility of verbal communication about the psychedelic experience. "Those who have taken a psychedelic drug realize it can't be talked about, and those who haven't naively assume that it can be talked about with the current vocabulary."

> Alpert, Metzner, and I were rookie pitchers being instructed by four veterans.

Coached Like Rookies

After the meeting, we met with four members of the institute who had previous experience with psychedelic drugs. Three were strangers, but without any social niceties, these men immediately plunged into a frank, avuncular coaching process, as though Alpert, Metzner, and I were rookie pitchers being instructed by four veterans; as though all seven of us were meeting to figure how to explain to earthlings the procedures and events of our totally different world.

Each coach had a different strategy. One said we should make our psychedelic lectures completely personal: "Tell concretely what happened to you." "Nonsense," said another. "Be strictly objective and scientific. Rely only on published data." A third disagreed: "Make it practical. Tell the audience about the dosage, how long it lasts, what people say and do during sessions." The fourth was the most psychological: "Recognize the fears of the listener. Anticipate his objections. Be humble. Stress the dangers and problems. Don't put him on the defensive."

> **Each coach had a different strategy.**

My Metaphor Rejected!

All four advisors were unanimous in criticizing my central metaphor: "'You have to go out of your mind to use your head,' is guaranteed to scare rational, intellectual people. Use a positive, familiar jargon. Talk about creative reorganization or perceptual reintegration."

> **You have to go out of your mind to use your head.**

But psychedelic drugs do take us beyond our normal conceptual framework. Most of the great religions have taken this disturbing goal of ex-stasis as their central program.

The experienced psychedelic veterans identified several fears generated by the psychedelic process which we saw as fear of the potential.

Fear of the Potential

Cognitive: Loss of rational control; fear of
   disorientation and confusion.

Social: Doing something shameful or   lu-
   dicrous; the loss of social inhibitions.

Psychological: Self-discovery; finding out
   something about yourself that you do not
   want to face.

Cultural: Discovering the painful truth about
   the institutions with which one is identified; seeing through the tribal shams;
   becoming disillusioned with one's social
   commitments and thus becoming irrespon-
   sible.

Ontological Addiction: Finding a new dimension of experience too pleasant; perhaps
   all men share the hunch that normal
   consciousness is a form of sleepwalking
   and that somewhere there exists a form
   of "awakeness" from which one would not
   want to return.

Illusion

Fear of losing the social-ego identity is based on an
illusion. One who has the courage to undergo the
shattering of the illusion will die, but in the mystical
sense, "so that he may live again." A Zen koan or paradox says: "Be dead, thoroughly dead, and do as you
will." The healing process, which Paul Tillich describes
as "taking a walk through hell," brings the transcen-

dence that lies beyond. Like other forms of anxiety, these five fears are related to deep yearnings and potentials. For each terror, there is a corresponding liberation. Terror is a negative desire. The terror of seeing yourself is the negative aspect of the ecstasy of really seeing yourself.

> For each terror, there is a corresponding liberation.

Chapter 14

New Language Needed

A science is born when a new tool is discovered for expanding the human sensorium—a new extension of the brain. The discovery of brain-change drugs has been compared to the discovery of the microscope. New forms swim into perception. It is a truism that you cannot impose the ethics and language of the past upon subject matter revealed by a new extension of the senses. Galileo was arrested for describing what he saw in his telescope. The Inquisition would not bother to look through the lens.

When Janssen, Galileo, Hooke, Leeuwenhoek, and Malpighi expanded human perception with the microscope, they realized that new languages, new theories were needed to use the new information. Our Harvard group of researchers argued for a new language to describe the expanded brain vistas triggered off by psychedelic drugs.

> **The discovery of brain-change drugs has been compared to the discovery of the microscope.**

S. I. Hayakawa, the well-known linguist, hated this idea. As editor of ETC, which published an article where I first advanced these thoughts, he wrote a solemn preface to the article where in which he claimed that his normal, routine perceptions were so full of sensation and freshness that he needed no expansion. He subsequently made fame and fortune politically espousing his conservative opposition to change. Sleepy Sam, as he was called, is one of the few psychological philosophers able to apply his knowledge of semantics and mass consciousness to real-life situations. More power to him!

Fixed on Externals

Mobile, far-ranging mammals have to pilot themselves through widely differing environments. Their complex machineries depend upon discrimination of cues and the learning of elaborate behavior sequences.

Consider the mammalian body as an enormous ocean liner with billions of passengers and crew—a completely self-contained, integrated, harmonious system of energy exchanges. But a look-out is required—of course—the so-called "waking consciousness," the mind.

Mammals complex machineries depend upon discrimination of cues and the learning of elaborate behavior sequences.

While millions of signals flood the mammalian cortex from all parts of the nervous system, one level of awareness has to be directed to the immediate external environment—to be alert to neighborhood changes, to distinguish between rewards and punishments, to select what is to be avoided and pursued. This neurological "fixing" on external cues is based on imprinting and subsequent conditioning.

Language Systems

Our bodies plod through complex energy fields, in-
capable of absorbing the largest part of the messages
surrounding us. But even so, the nervous system is still
capable of a much wider range of awareness. Tantric
Hinduism, for example, suggests that a universe of
awareness exists at each of seven chakras, or nerve
centers, in the body. For centuries Oriental psychologists have been developing methods to activate these
chakra levels.

Reality Upside Down

Our restriction of consciousness is, of course, no set-
back to the genetic blueprint. Life (DNA) is transmitted
by us, through us, even though we sleepwalk. Perhaps
the duties of the hive require a blindness to broader
meanings and rapturous vibrations.

In his book, All and Everything, George I. Gurdjieff
suggests that if man saw his true position in the evolutionary sequence, he might in despair quit playing his
role. In order to keep man chasing externals, Gurdjieff
speculates, the Kundabuffer organ—clearly a brilliant
anticipation of the concept of imprinting—was introduced into the nervous system to keep man attached
to external striving and cause him to see reality upside
down.

Illusion of Communication

**The absurdity
of language is
now clear.**

The absurdity of language is
now clear. Each of us labors
under the illusion that our imprint board is reality—a situation beautifully described by

Plato's Cave, or the parable of The Blind Men and the Elephant. When two human beings attempt to communicate, the absurdity is compounded—my chessboard interacting with your Monopoly game.

Those who live at the same time and in the same anthill share enough consensual codes to preserve the illusion of communication. That fraction of our language that refers to visible events in local space-time is reasonably efficient. We can communicate about static externals and materials, but little else.

There is a natural tendency to impose the language and rituals of the past upon new experience. As an inevitable fallout of my profession as encourager and stimulator of creative singularity, can you imagine the range of letters I receive in any week? From freaky, tormented prophets and visionaries in Kansas City, Nome, Melbourne, and Cape Town-souls who "see," "experience" "know" certain truths, and who breathlessly describe these revelations in tired vocabularies, using CIA conspiracies, UFO visitations, and reincarnation cliches—invariably Egyptian, to threaten whoever fails to accept the valid new connections perceived by their mistimed, out-of-phase futique brains.

> Those who live at the same time and in the same anthill share enough consensual codes to preserve the illusion of communication.

Improving Linguistic Systems

There are three ways to improve man's linguistic system. First, we can increase our current imprint's efficiency by recognizing clearly what we have imprinted, recognizing our chessboard's limitations and dimensions, and developing new chains of association to open up the imprint board, without brain-change drugs.

A second possibility is to suspend the imprint with drugs, and tune in on the internal and external energy accessible to the human nervous system. Western psychology recognizes no methods or possibilities for getting off the imprint board. We must work within the tribal, temporary, accidental limits.

Reimprint carefully, selecting the new chessboard, choosing the persons and externals to which we will become voluntarily hooked.

Note that suspension of imprint is temporary. No one has yet demonstrated the possibility of remaining "high" indefinitely. The problem of re-entry, return to externals, must always be met. Therefore the third approach to improving our linguistic system is to reimprint carefully, selecting the new chessboard, choosing the persons and externals to which we will become voluntarily hooked.

Communicating the Internal

We can learn from the physical sciences, which keep their language system in tune with the processes they measure. A chemical formula is a functional shorthand that words can never reproduce. The linguistics of the chemical formula allow us to make changes in the formula that parallel changes in molecular structure.

As Ilya Prigogine suggests, evolution involves dissipative structures. Nature is an open system, and any denotation describing nature should strive for openness as well. The philosophic advances stimulated by the physical sciences will inevitably filter down and be incorporated into a culture's communication. Everyone now babbles about "feedback" or "noise" or "input." This may improve communication about external affairs, but not the problem of communicating the internal, the experiential.

Language Shapes Experience

When we deal with the neurological, we dip our cups into the rushing stream of experience. "Reality" is always subjective, unique, and irreplicable; "truth" subjective, unique, and fleeting. Since language determines experience, we must design a language that distinguishes the external from the neurological experience. If our language is closed, so will be our experiencing, perception, and thinking.

> **If our language is closed, so will be our experiencing, perception, and thinking.**

But some system is necessary. If our linguistic structure is chaotic and haphazard, then so will be our thinking and experiencing. The recent popularity of YMCA-Hindu-Buddhist babble is an ominous example of mushiness.

Experiential Language

To describe internal neurological events, three types of experiential languages are possible. We can use external symbols to describe our experiencing, but only when consciousness is completely externalized, tied to external references—only one very limited type of experiencing.

We can use external symbols to describe our experiencing, but only when consciousness is completely externalized.

Alternatively, we can combine external symbols in novel subjective forms—creative, imaginative, fantasized, visionary thinking. Such experiencing is pathological if involuntary—hallucinations, delusions; highly valued as poetic, when voluntary. We experience in terms of familiar external symbols, but combine them in novel ways.

A third approach is to bypass symbols completely. Communicate in terms of the energy recorded by our nervous system. We communicate these experiences by selecting and directing audio-visual energy sources that stimulate the nervous system of the person to whom we are communicating.

Experiential Vocabulary

In developing an experiential vocabulary we can include all the terms of the "old language," but the words no longer denote external movements in space-time. They are buzzwords with no external reference, just metaphorical noises, that activate an experience and hopefully communicate my buzz to someone else.

Don't worry about external logic when you are metaphorically describing experience: the sentence, "it was a solid-gold, billion-dollar orgasm" does not involve a transaction that your stuffy banker will honor.

If you are describing an external game sequence, you must, on the contrary, be prudishly conscientious about the semantics of movements in space-time. If you plan to communicate internal states metaphorically, using external symbols—including words—you must smash through linguistic conventions—alter sequences, turn words upside down, cut up and reassemble verbal sequences from all relevant sources.

> **If you are describing an external game sequence, you must be prudishly conscientious about the semantics of movements in space-time.**

Chapter 15

Developing Creativity

Until recently, no psychologist could explain why genius emerges and how it could be nurtured. Or, even more unthinkable, how genius could be produced-because this implies improving the species beyond the level of the hive leaders. A paper on creativity which I wrote in the barbarous period circa 1962, emphasized one's choice over one's own behavior and brain changes.

To describe externals, you become a scientist. To describe experience, you become an artist. The old distinction between artists and scientists must vanish. Every time we teach a child correct usage of an external symbol, we must spend as much time teaching him how to fission and reassemble external grammar to communicate the internal.

To describe externals, you become a scientist. To describe experience, you become an artist.

The training of artists and creative performers can be a straightforward, almost mechanical process. When you teach someone how to perform creatively (i.e., associate dead symbols in new combinations), you expand his potential for experiencing more widely and richly.

Binocular Approach

Johnny is assigned an essay on "A Day at the County Fair." He writes an essay like a police-evidence report. Accurate observation tells him about external movements on the fairgrounds. He is then assigned to write: "My Experience at the County Fair." Here he reassembles the jumble of smells, sounds, memories, images in the style of James Joyce or William Burroughs.

Every word in the dictionary can be combined in endlessly new sequences. Every paragraph in the encyclopedia or any other publication becomes a paint pot in which we can dip our experiential brush. Photographs, paintings, objects, can be reassembled into new forms to express an experience nonverbally. The work of Bruce Conner, the eccentric garbage-can assembler is a good example. On his painting board, Conner nails a burlesque poster, a worn-out brassiere, a faded hat-feather, a tattered perfume ad. He covers the whole with transparent nylon hosiery and communicates the poignancy of sexual disillusionment.

This technique could be taught in primary school. In art class, Johnny is told to describe a flower; then

A binocular technique could be taught in primary school.

is asked to cut up and reassemble to communicate his experience of the flower. This binocular approach to education teaches the philosophic distinction between "subject matter" and "reality," between objective, consensual "fact' and subjective "truth."

Beyond External Language

The vocabulary of external reference covers the most prosaic and game-limited fragment of experience. We play with a very limited

We play with a very limited set of Sears, Roebuck symbols.

set of Sears, Roebuck symbols. Korzybski suggested increasing semantic breadth and accuracy by a numerical code: instead of "apple," we have apple^1, apple^2, etc. Combining and reassembling words also multiplies their expressive potential, but we are still left with a lexicography basically designed for describing visible, objective space-time movements.

Language of Games

But experience is widely subjective. It transcends games. In constructing a vocabulary and grammar of internal reactions, where do we begin? One starting place is the language of games that claim to be transcendental or experiential. Philosophies of the East are concerned with the internal, i.e., the neurological. Their ontologies, epistemologies, and logics are the despair of the Western scholar attuned to an external philosophy.

We are told that Sanskrit, compared to English, contains about forty times the number of references to experiential events. It is no accident that most non-psychiatric researchers in the psychedelic field found it useful to borrow the terminology of Oriental philosophy. But it is pointless to teach our children experiential Sanskrit, because it is still a language of words, far removed from the speed and flow of experience.

Transcending Verbal-Symbol Imprinting

To experience directly, we must transcend the verbal-symbol imprint, experience energy-flow directly, receive energy messages directly. The future language of experience will be based directly on the concepts and technology of light, sound, cellular movement, sympathetic and parasympathetic nervous system imagery: direct replication of energy flow.

Consciousness is a biochemical neurological decoding that takes place at many levels of the nervous system. Units of the language will be based on units for measuring and describing these energy transformations.

In the 21st century, we shall all talk like physicists. Communication about external events is science. All men are good or bad scientists when they describe external events. But men must become artists to describe internal events.

We ostracize those who try to turn us on—by social isolation, censorship, and legal restrictions.

In developing systems for communicating experience, how can we transmit energy patterns to "turn on" the receiver—i.e., directly stimulate the nervous system, bypassing the receiver's symbol system? Most of us are terrified by free neurological energy. We resist being turned on. We ostracize those who try to turn us on—by social isolation, censorship, and legal restrictions.

Hive Symbol System

The consensual symbolic hallucination must be maintained. Any rent in the hive symbol system threatens the structural delusion. While the illustrator is welcomed, the buzz-shock artist—who turns you on—is anathematized by the conventional hive member.

> Any rent in the hive symbol system threatens the structural delusion.

The creative artist's aim is the same as the scientist's: accurate recording of the dance of energy transformations. The scientist observes the external, the artist the experienced. The engineer manipulates the external, the illustrator portrays it. Neither is an artist.

Chapter 16

Artistic Language Systems

Reproductive Art focuses only on the external, hive-consensual, static symbolical structure-the game. Great illustrators, like Norman Rockwell and Durer, succeed in communicating the revealing epiphany moments of game culmination. By contrast, Visionary Art, also called neosymbolic art, attempts to translate the energy dance in terms of unique combinations of static symbols. Examples include Hieronymus Bosch, Lenora Carrington, Goya, the Surrealists, Dali, John Cage, Antonio Gaudio Transcendental Art or Tranart, by comparison, avoids reliance on familiar symbols or external forms and directly transmits sensory energy. Abstract art is a step in this direction.

Beyond the hive imprint all is one dance of electrical energy, of cellular process.

Physics, biology, biochemistry, genetics, and Tranart all express the same message: Beyond the hive imprint, all is one dance of electrical energy, of cellular process. Science and art have the same aim: to record the process.

Constant Whirling Change

We have been taught to narrow our awareness to a fantasy world of symbol solids. But that's not how it really is. All matter is energy—everything is whirling change, even you! Look at your baby pictures. Look in the mirror. You are a dramatically changing process.

All matter is energy— everything is whirling change, even you!

Imagine a mile-high camera taking a picture of your city every six months. Run six hundred frames through your projector. Representative art plays the delusionary game with familiar static categories. Visionary art invents its own categories. Tranart attempts to get back to the cortical flash. Op art, for example, attempts to return to the retina, freezing the naked, patternless mosaic. Your Persian rug—the Islamic artist is forbidden to reproduce forms—is static Tranart, an unstained experiential slide of retinal sensation.

Have you seen a cross-section of retinal tissue? A many-layered technicolor swamp of rods and cones, interlaced with capillaries. No Sears, Roebuck images there! Imagine your Persian rug undulating, each unit in motion, a swirling rock-and-roll of color. That's what the original rug designers had in mind. The rug contains the message, the reminder.

Reproductive art reminds only that man can share static symbols. Illustrative painting and photography freeze the symbolic. Abstract painting and microscopic photographs freeze the process. Moving pictures help keep the hallucinatory process going and duplicate the imprinted "reality" delusion.

In the latter half of the 20th century we witnessed the emergence of psychedelic Tranart attempts to communicate nonsymbolically, to cut through hallucinations to the direct sensation, to produce the direct sensation of flowing process, a reproduction of the microscopic event.

Psychedelic Tranart

Psychedelic drugs provide creative experience-suspending verbal governors so that the neurological motor operates at high speed. To communicate a psychedelic experience, you require psychedelic Tranart, which tries to keep up with the speed and breadth of direct sensation.

> **Psychedelic drugs provide creative experience-suspending verbal governors so that the neurological motor operates at high speed.**

After psychedelic training, we accustom ourselves to the pace of the nervous system. We experience a flood of new worlds. Tranart requires new technical means, based on the machines now used by scientists, to record (1) the life process, (2) the energy dance.

Instead of the brush and the Leica, psychedelic artists use the electromicroscopic camera, random analog projectors, multiple films and tapes, polarized light, chemically treated slides, the oscilloscope, the telescopic camera, lasers, computer animation, sci-fi special effects.

LSD Pushes the Artistic Envelope

Conventional visual art techniques involve the surface, such as a canvas or paper, the paint or covering substance,
and the instruments, such as a palette knife, or brush, to shape the design. Tranart employs the same three media—the screen, which can vary in shape and texture—the energy source is always changing. These energy patterns are called *Direct Process Images* (DPI's); and symbolic representations are called *Learned Form Images* (LFI's).

With tranart the energy source is always changing.

Direct process images externalize representations of the flow of direct sensation-experience. Flowing, unstructured, unidentifiable—they are communications of the experience of direct energy. Learned form images are representations of learned and artifactual perceptual forms: objects, things, organisms, events, bodies, chairs, flowers. Both direct process images and learned form images may be auditory or visual, internal or external, depending on whether they represent experiences bubbling out of the lower nervous system or coming from without.

Thus, *visual internal* direct process images are moving magnifications of retinal processes—cellular or subcellular events—organic direct process images. Visual external direct process images are moving pictures of energy processes at the atomic or subatomic level—waves, interacting planes of light, images of inorganic processes continually moving, flowing, dancing.

There are also auditory direct process images—recordings of sounds heard from inside of the body, which is internal and recordings of sounds registered in the brain without cognitive patternings, unstructured natural white noise, which is external.

Chapter 17

Three Kinds of Art

Visual learned form images are representations of "things" if they are consensual and representations of "hallucinations" if idiosyncratic. Traditional moving pictures and filmed sequences are visual learned form images. So symphonies are auditory learned form images—game sequences for the trained ear. Auditory internal learned form images are representations of experiences generally considered psychotic such as hearing "voices" or meaningful" sounds inside your head.

Thus, we have three kinds of art communicating three types of experiences. First is "reality-oriented" art which includes story-telling, reproductive, realistic art. In the second old images are combined into new patterns, blending incongruous sequences. The montage, assemblage, the movie "cut-up" method used by Bruce Conner in which he recombines dozens of old newsreels is an example. Salvador Dali's surrealistic combinations of organic and inorganic forms and John Cage's chance combinations of sounds and noises also fall into this category.

Neurological Tranart which records the mixture and interweaving of direct process with learned game form, is the third kind of art. Examples include Van Gogh's skies, which contain energy vortices, and Tchelitchew's *Hide and Seek* with its mysterious faces moving out of capillary streams and organic networks. Visionary Sufi miniatures have rocks in the backgrounds which, when you look closely, seem to have mysterious faces hidden in them. Bruce Conner's Cosmic Ray movie is another example: it has pulsing abstract forms out of which emerge now a naked woman, now marching soldiers, now parachutes, now Mickey Mouse. Visionary Tranart is learned form images imposed on or woven into direct process images. Game concepts are superimposed on the energy process.

Pure Tranart attempts to record pure, symbol-free energy. Jackson Pollock's paintings are indistinguishable from retinal cross sections. Persian rugs are only slightly more symmetrical. To represent visual internal direct process images, we used recurrent film loops of microbiological processes. When projected, these uncannily reproduce the

"What is it?" That's the point, of course!

psychedelic vision. Cells dance through technicolor swamps. Ciliated protoplasm flails down undulating channels. Membrane spheres bounce across vague tissue landscapes, flowing without cease.

"What is it?" That's the point, of course! You can't label the microscopic process with macroscopic terms. The cellular life signals never stop. The film keeps moving.

Direct Process Image Library

Tranart requires a wide variety of paint-color or sound-notes. A library of visual direct process images is a collection of slides and films of energy and microbiological life processes. Just as the painter knows the range of available pigments, so the Tranartist knows the range of available direct process images representing direct, formless sensations.

> Just as the painter knows the range of available pigments, so the Tranartist knows the range of available direct process images representing direct, formless sensations.

More Useful Than Words

After your visions, you select from the direct process images film catalogue the closest representation. No direct process image comes close to direct sensation, of course, but it comes closer than words. The very existence of a direct process image lexicon lets you know where to go for a more exact representation. Microbiological film technicians and physics-lab technicians thus become the philologists of the new direct process images language.

Learned Form Image Library

In neosymbolic or visionary Tranart, structure is provided by learned form images—films or tape-recordings of structured events, objects, people. For example, researchers at the Castalia Foundation developed a code system for every cultural, personal, biological, and chemical event. When a structured or consensual hallucination sequence—visual, auditory, tactual—is needed to add form to a Tranart communication, a filmstrip is located in the learned form image library, or created.

> **With infinite combinations of experiential images, it is possible to express any experience of noncultural energy, life process, or visionary creation.**

Infinite Combinations

An ever-increasing library of catalogued direct process images and learned form images is thus assembled. With infinite combinations of experiential images, it is possible to express any experience of noncultural energy, life process, or visionary creation. To record a visionary experience—a mixture of primary process and cultural sequence—requires Visionary Tranart—learned form images imposed on or woven into direct process images.

Visionary Tranart

A vision of undulating streams or bouncing spheres, which are not recognized as blood cells, converts as a learned form image is imposed on the primary process into uncoiling serpent-flow, which changes to a network of Chinese Communist soldiers, which shifts into the florid, pulsating face of a leering Oriental dictator which flickers into the portrait of one's feared stepmother.

A blood-circulation direct process image film loop is set running on one projector. Then the subject finds a learned form image sequence of uncoiling serpents. They are green, so he imposes a red filter. The direct process image projector starts running and after a minute the red-filter-serpent learned form image projector is snapped on—out of focus.

Gradually, the learned form image strip is brought into focus and the vision slowly shifts from pure direct process images to DPI/LFI vision. The learned form image filmstrip is then spliced to newsreel film of marching Chinese columns, and then the picture of Chou En-lai. A still photo of Stepmother is inserted in a slide projector with a veined red filter completely out of focus and slowly focused at the appropriate second.

The Tranartist experiments until he gets the flowing sequence he wants, with learned form images fading in and out of focus—with the pulsing Direct process images stream always flowing, flowing in the background. Then he adds sound.

The pump of a heartbeat fades into the thud of marching feet, to shouted commands in Chinese, to Stepmother's voice screaming "You'll never amount to anything."

The pump of a heartbeat fades into the thud of marching feet, to shouted commands in Chinese, to Stepmother's voice screaming "You'll never amount to anything." The sound sequence is adjusted to the visual barrage and speeded up—30 seconds of the Tranart representation of a psychedelic vision.

No Limits

Perceived forms swim into focus out of the swirling, unformed wave process—a fact of perception. Visionary Tranart makes it possible to duplicate this as an expressed communication. In principle, there is no limit to the range of DPI/LFI communication. Tranart is based on the raw records of science, which become part of a new and vastly expanded basic language of experience.

Tranart is based on the raw records of science, which become part of a new and vastly expanded basic language of experience.

Language approaches the speed and extension of the neural network, an increasing percentage of which becomes available to consciousness, communication, and conceptualization.

Ronin Books for Independent Minds

9 781579 510176